KU-610-787

CONTENTS

INTRODUCTION

This book is full of cross-stitch designs featuring charming country cottages, which are depicted in a variety of ways to suit both beginners and dedicated stitchers.

The designs have been chosen to illustrate the variety of the traditional cottage. From the tiny designs to hang on the Christmas tree, to the comprehensive picture of the village with its mix of cottages along the narrow street leading up to the church, there is a design to suit everyone's taste. Beads and silver and gold threads have been used to give greater depth to the designs, which can be used as pictures, cushions, table linen, and Christmas decorations.

Each project is beautifully illustrated with a full-colour picture, and accompanied by clear stitch charts, and full details for completing the cross-stitch items. Cross stitch is very simple to do and, with the help of the comprehensive Basic Skills section of the book, even complete beginners will find many of the designs suitable for a first project.

Whatever your cross-stitching experience, you will find both inspiration and variety as you browse through the pages of this book. I hope you enjoy recreating these designs and bringing the charm of cottage life into your home.

Happy Stitching!

BASIC SKILLS

BEFORE YOU BEGIN

PREPARING THE FABRIC

Even with an average amount of handling, many evenweave fabrics tend to fray at the edges, so it is a good idea to overcast the raw edges, using ordinary sewing thread, before you begin.

FABRIC

Many of the projects in this book use 14-count Aida fabric, which has a surface of 14 clearly defined squares or 'blocks' of threads per 2.5cm (1in). This fabric is produced by Zweigart. Evenweave fabrics — 25-count and 28-count — are also used; these have the same number of warp and weft threads per 2.5cm (1in), and stitches are taken over two threads in each direction.

THE INSTRUCTIONS

Each project begins with a full list of the materials that you will require. The measurements given for the embroidery fabric include a minimum of 5cm (2in) all around to allow for stretching it in a frame and preparing the edges to prevent them from fraying.

Colour keys for stranded embroidery cottons — Anchor, DMC or Madeira — are given with each chart. It is assumed that you will need to buy one skein of each colour mentioned in a particular key, even though you may use less, but where two or more skeins are needed, this information is included in the main list of requirements.

Before you begin to embroider, always mark the centre of the design with two lines of basting stitches, one vertical and one horizontal, running from edge to edge of the fabric, as indicated by the arrows on the charts.

As you stitch, use the centre lines given on the chart and the basting threads on your fabric as reference points for counting the squares and threads to position your design accurately.

WORKING IN A HOOP

A hoop is the most popular frame for use with small areas of embroidery. It consists of two rings, one fitted inside the other; the outer ring usually has an adjustable screw attachment so that it can be tight-

Traditional Cottages
IN CROSS STITCH

Angela Beazley

For cottage lovers everywhere. Whether you
live in one or not, here's to their character,
and their sheer inconvenience.

THE CHARTS

Some of the designs in this book are very detailed and, due to inevitable space limitations, the charts may be shown on a comparatively small scale; in such cases, readers may find it helpful to have the particular chart enlarged.

THREADS

The projects in this book were all stitched with Anchor stranded cotton embroidery threads. The keys given with each chart also list thread combinations for those who wish to use DMC or Madeira threads. It should be pointed out that the shades produced by different companies vary slightly, and it is not always possible to find identical colours in a different range.

Published in 1998 by Merehurst Limited
Ferry House, 51-57 Lacy Road, Putney, London SW15 1PR
Copyright © 1998 Merehurst Limited
ISBN 1 85391 721 4

A catalogue record for this book is available from the British Library.

Edited by Heather Dewhurst
Designed by Maggie Aldred
Photography by Juliet Piddington
Illustrations by John Hutchinson
Colour separation by Bright Arts (HK) Ltd
Printed in Hong Kong by Wing King Tong

Merehurst is the leading publisher of craft books and has an excellent range of titles to suit all levels. Please send to the address above for our free catalogue, stating the title of this book.

ened to hold the stretched fabric in place. Hoops are available in several sizes, ranging from 10cm (4in) in diameter to quilting hoops with a diameter of 38cm (15in). Hoops with table stands or floor stands attached are also available.

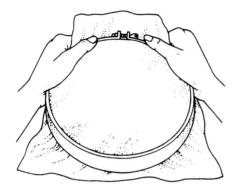

1 To stretch your fabric in a hoop, place the area to be embroidered over the inner ring and press the outer ring over it, with the tension screw released. Tissue paper can be placed between the outer ring and the embroidery, so that the hoop does not mark the fabric. Lay the tissue paper over the fabric when you set it in the hoop, then tear away the central embroidery area.

2 Smooth the fabric and, if necessary, straighten the grain before tightening the screw. The fabric should be evenly stretched.

WORKING IN A RECTANGULAR FRAME
Rectangular frames are more suitable for larger pieces of embroidery. They consist of two rollers, with tapes attached, and two flat side pieces, which slot into the rollers and are held in place by pegs or screw attachments. Available in different sizes, either alone or with adjustable table or floor stands, frames are measured by the length of the roller tape, and range in size from 30cm (12in) to 68cm (27in).

As alternatives to a slate frame, canvas stretchers and the backs of old picture frames can be used. Provided there is sufficient extra fabric around the finished size of the embroidery, the edges can be

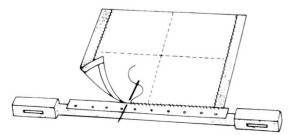

turned under and simply attached with drawing pins (thumb tacks) or staples.

1 To stretch your fabric in a rectangular frame, cut out the fabric, allowing at least an extra 5cm (2in) all around the finished size of the embroidery. Baste a single 12mm (1/2in) turning on the top and bottom edges and oversew strong tape, 2.5cm (1in) wide, to the other two sides. Mark the centre line both ways with basting stitches. Working from the centre outward and using strong thread, oversew the top and bottom edges to the roller tapes. Fit the side pieces into the slots and roll any extra fabric on one roller until the fabric is taut.

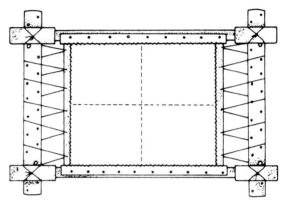

2 Insert the pegs or adjust the screw attachments to secure the frame. Thread a large-eyed needle (chenille needle) with strong thread or fine string and lace both edges, securing the ends around the intersections of the frame. Lace the webbing at 2.5cm (1in) intervals, stretching the fabric evenly.

EXTENDING EMBROIDERY FABRIC
It is easy to extend a piece of embroidery fabric, such as a bookmark, to stretch it in a hoop.

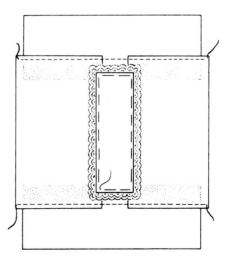

• Fabric oddments of a similar weight can be used. Simply cut four pieces to size (in other words, to the measurement that will fit both the embroidery fabric and your hoop) and baste them to each side of the embroidery fabric before stretching it in the hoop in the usual way.

THE STITCHES

CROSS STITCH

For all cross stitch embroidery, the following two methods of working are used. In each case, neat rows of vertical stitches are produced on the back of the fabric.

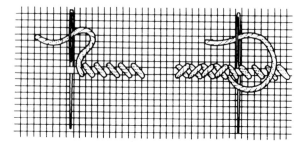

• When stitching large areas, work in horizontal rows. Working from right to left, complete the first row of evenly spaced diagonal stitches over the number of threads specified in the project instructions. Then, working from left to right, repeat the process. Continue in this way, making sure each stitch crosses in the same direction.

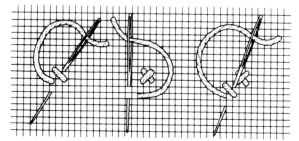

• When stitching diagonal lines, work downwards, completing each stitch before moving on to the next. When starting a project, always begin to embroider at the centre of the design and work outwards to ensure that the design will be placed centrally on the fabric.

BACKSTITCH

Backstitch is used in the projects to give emphasis to a particular foldline, an outline or a shadow. The stitches are worked over the same number of

threads as the cross stitch, forming continuous straight or diagonal lines.

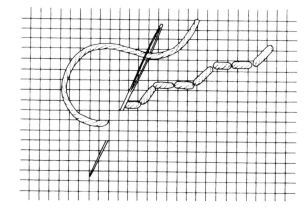

• Make the first stitch from left to right; pass the needle behind the fabric and bring it out one stitch length ahead to the left. Repeat and continue in this way along the line.

THREE-QUARTER CROSS STITCH

Some fractional stitches are used on certain projects in this book; although they strike fear into the hearts of less experienced stitchers they are not difficult to master, and give a more natural line in certain instances. Should you find it difficult to pierce the centre of the Aida block, simply use a sharp needle to make a small hole in the centre first.

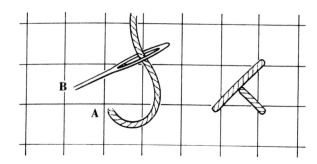

To work a three-quarter cross stitch, bring the needle up at point A and down through the centre of the square at B. Later, a diagonal backstitch finishes the stitch. A chart square with two different symbols separated by a diagonal line requires two 'three-quarter' stitches. Backstitch will later finish the square.

TENT STITCH

Tent stitch is worked diagonally over only one intersection of the canvas and the needle always covers at least two threads on the wrong side of the work. It looks similar to half cross stitch from the front of the stitching, but from the back it produces long sloping stitches whereas half cross stitch has vertical stitches.

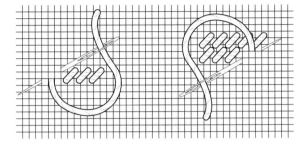

To work tent stitch, start at the top right and work from right to left. Start with the needle behind the fabric, bring it out through a square, then take it diagonally over one intersection to the upper right. Then bring it out in the square to the left of the first stitch and take it down diagonally over one intersection to the upper right. Continue across the fabric in the same way.

BEADING
Using beads in cross stitch gives added texture to a design. Use one strand of stranded cotton in the needle. Knot the end of the cotton, and come up in the middle of the first square you wish to place a bead in. Make two small stitches in the square and then come up at the lower left hole in that square. Your thread is now secured and you are ready to make the first bead stitch. Secure the bead in place by using a half cross stitch, working from the lower left to the top right of the Aida fabric.

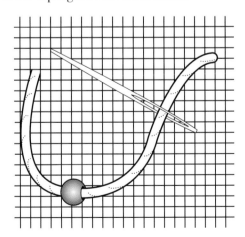

MOUNTING EMBROIDERY
The cardboard should be cut to the size of the finished embroidery, with an extra amount added all round to allow for the recess in the frame.

LIGHTWEIGHT FABRICS

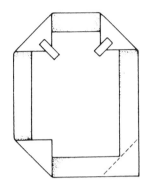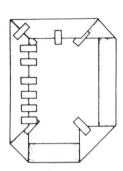

1 Place the embroidery face down, with the cardboard centred on top, and basting and pencil lines matching. Begin by folding over the fabric at each corner and securing it with masking tape.

2 Working first on one side and then the other, fold over the fabric on all sides and secure it firmly with pieces of masking tape, placed about 2.5cm (1in) apart. Neaten the mitred corners with masking tape too, pulling the fabric tightly to give a firm, smooth finish.

HEAVIER FABRICS

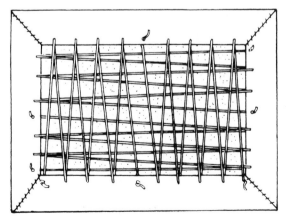

Lay the embroidery face down, with the cardboard centred on top; fold over the edges of the fabric on opposite sides, making mitred folds at the corners, and lace across, using strong thread. Repeat on the other two sides. Finally, pull up the fabric firmly over the cardboard. Overstitch the mitred corners.

Cottage Garden Table Set

This colourful project will bring summer flowers to your table all the year around. Both the place mat and the pair of coasters are quick to make and suitable for beginners.

COTTAGE GARDEN TABLE SET

YOU WILL NEED

For the Place Mat, with a finished size of
35cm x 29cm (14in x 11¹/₂in):

*41cm x 33cm (16in x 13in) of ivory 28-count
evenweave fabric
Stranded embroidery cotton in the colours
given in the panel
No24 and No26 tapestry needles*

For the Coasters, with a design area measuring
6.5cm (2¹/₂in) square:

*35cm x 18cm (14in x 7¹/₄in) of white 18-count
Aida fabric
Stranded embroidery cotton in the colours
given in the panel
No26 tapestry needle
Cream embroidery thread
Acrylic coaster, 8cm (3¹/₄in) round
Acrylic coaster, 8cm (3¹/₄in) square*

●

THE PLACE MAT

Prepare the fabric, basting the horizontal and vertical centre lines, following the instructions given on page 4. Set the fabric in a hoop or frame, and begin stitching from the centre, following the chart. Ensure that the long axis of the fabric is running horizontally.

Work the cross stitch using two strands of thread in the No24 tapestry needle, and working over two threads of the fabric in each direction to form a cross stitch. Make sure that all the top stitches run in the same direction. Work the backstitch using one strand of thread and the No26 needle.

HEMSTITCHING

To finish the place mat, remove the embroidery from the frame. Trim the fabric to the finished size, being careful to remove an equal amount of fabric from each of the four sides. Count twelve threads in from the raw edges, and remove one thread on each of the four sides. This forms the hem line. Take two

▶ PLACE MAT	ANCHOR	DMC	MADEIRA
2 Light salmon pink	1022	760	0405
3 Dark salmon pink	1023	3712	0406
↑ Pale yellow	293	727	0110
⊓ Sand	373	3828	2102
E Dark sand	374	420	2103
H Maroon	43	815	0513
L Medium green	266	3347	1408
O Bright yellow	295	726	0100
/ Light grey green	875	503	1702
S Dark grey green	876	502	1703
T Bright green	241	954	1211
V Brick	883	3064	2312
N Grey blue	849	927	1708
Z Dark blue	851	924	1706
+ Purple	98	553	0712
Dark brown*	381	838	1914

Note: Bks flower detail with maroon, and cottage detail, including windows, with dark brown* (*used for backstitch only); follow the small chart showing large cross stitches.

▶ COASTERS	ANCHOR	DMC	MADEIRA
• Light stone	391	3024	1901
2 Dark brick	883	3064	2312
3 Light brick	882	3773	2313
S Grey blue	850	926	1707
E Grey brown	903	3032	2002
= Dark grey	8581	646	1812
↑ Light grey	900	648	1814
⊓ Light grey*	900	648	1814
H Dark green	217	319	1313
L Medium green	215	320	1311
N Pink	50	3716	0612
T Light yellow	293	727	0110
V Light sage green	262	3051	1508
Z Dark pink	42	961	0610
Y Dark blue	851	924	1706

Note: Bks details with one strand of dark grey. Work smoke in light grey* using tent stitch (*tent stitch only).

strands of cream embroidery thread in the No24 needle and begin to hem as follows.

Starting from the bottom left-hand corner, bring the needle out on the right side of the work, four threads inside the drawn thread line. Working from left to right, pick up four threads. Bring the needle

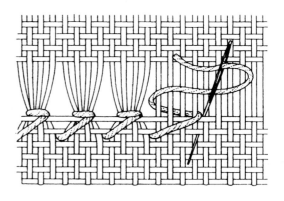

▲ *Place mat*

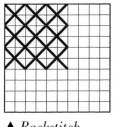

▲ *Backstitch window design*

Coasters ▶

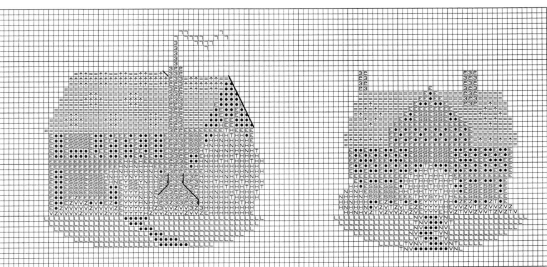

out again and insert it behind the fabric to emerge four threads along ready to make the next stitch. Before inserting the needle, pull the thread tight, so that the bound threads form a neat group. If you have never worked this stitch before you might like to practise on a spare piece of fabric first. When you have finished hemstitching the place mat, pull away the threads outside the hem for a frayed edge.

THE COASTERS

Prepare the fabric by dividing it into two squares measuring 18cm (7^1/$_4$in) each, and centring them as before. Set the fabric in a hoop or frame and begin stitching from the centre. Work all stitches with one strand of thread in the No26 needle. To finish, trim the fabric to fit the coaster exactly, and assemble as shown in the assembly instructions.

11

The Cottage Kitchen

This cosy cottage kitchen, with its old-fashioned sink and dresser laden with crockery, invites you to step in and warm yourself by the range. The stitched patchwork border tells us there is an embroiderer living here.

THE COTTAGE KITCHEN

YOU WILL NEED

For the Picture, with a design area of
16cm x 11cm (6¼in x 4¼in):

30cm x 25cm (12in x 10in) of light green,
14-count Aida fabric
Stranded embroidery cotton in the colours
given in the panel
No24 and No26 tapestry needles
Cardboard and masking tape for mounting
Frame of your choice

•

THE EMBROIDERY

Prepare the fabric, basting the horizontal and vertical centre lines, following the instructions given on
page 4. Set the fabric in a hoop or frame, and begin
stitching from the centre, following the chart.
Ensure that the long axis of the fabric is running
horizontally.

Work the cross stitch using two strands of thread
in the No24 tapestry needle and cross-stitching over
one block of the fabric. Make sure that all the top
stitches run in the same direction. Work the backstitch details using one strand of thread and the
No26 needle.

▶ COTTAGE KITCHEN		ANCHOR	DMC	MADEIRA
•	White	01	Blanc	White
L	Dark pine green	879	500	1705
=	Dark grey	400	317	1714
■	Black	403	310	Black
T	Rust	349	301	2306
Z	Dark sand	374	420	2103
E	Light pine green	859	523	1509
V	Medium pine green	262	3051	1602
+	Brick	883	3064	2312
H	Brown	358	433	2008
↑	Grass green	265	471	1501
S	Pale blue	128	827	1014
▼	Red	19	347	0407
3	Pale yellow	300	746	0101
K	Light sand	373	3828	2102
N	Heather	872	3041	0806
	Very dark grey*	401	535	1809

*Note: Bks round the cat with black. Bks all other details with very
dark grey* (*used for backstitch only).*

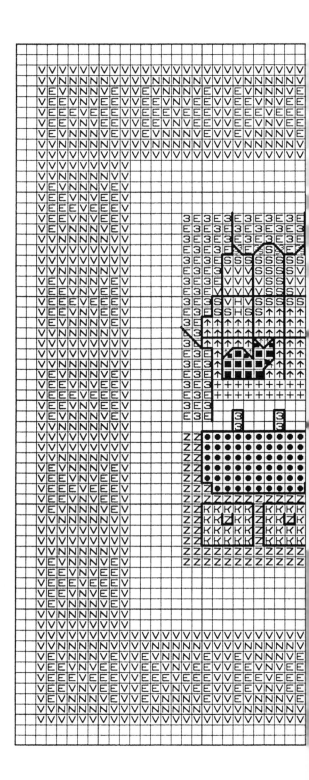

FINISHING

Remove the embroidery from the frame. Gently
hand wash the embroidery if desired. Press on the
reverse side with a warm steam iron.

Mount as shown in the Basic Skills section on page 7, following the instructions for lightweight fabrics. Insert the mounted picture into the frame according to the manufacturer's instructions.

The High Street

This charming design shows a variety of cottage styles set in a village high street in spring. The cottages are complemented by delicate pink blossom on the trees, and front gardens full of colourful flowers.

THE HIGH STREET

YOU WILL NEED

For the Picture, with a design area of
21.5cm x 8.5cm (8¼in x 3½in):

*41cm x 29cm (16¼in x 11½in) of light blue,
28-count evenweave fabric
Stranded embroidery cotton in the colours
given in the panel
No24 and No26 tapestry needles
Strong thread for lacing across the back
Cardboard, for mounting
Frame of your choice*

THE EMBROIDERY

Prepare the fabric, basting the horizontal and vertical lines, following the instructions given on page 4. Set the fabric in a hoop or frame, and begin stitching from the centre, following the chart. Ensure that the long axis of the fabric is running horizontally.

Work the cross stitch over two threads of fabric using two strands of thread in the No24 tapestry needle. Make sure that all the top stitches run in the same direction. Work the backstitch details using one strand of cotton in the No26 needle.

FINISHING

Remove the embroidery from the frame. Gently hand wash the embroidery if desired. Press on the reverse side with a warm steam iron. Mount as shown in the Basic Skills section on page 7, following the instructions for heavier fabrics. Insert the mounted picture into the frame according to the manufacturer's instructions.

▼ THE HIGH STREET		ANCHOR	DMC	MADEIRA
E	Grey	398	318	1802
L	Cream	386	3823	0102
H	Pale pink	893	225	0814
T	Maroon	44	814	0514
2	Light brick	882	3773	2313
↑	Dark brick	883	3064	2312
3	Rust	349	301	2306
O	Dark emerald green	210	562	1206
•	Emerald green	208	912	1207
=	Bright brown	357	975	2304
N	Light brown	370	434	2303
▼	Light sand	373	3828	2102
S	Dark sand	374	420	2103
Y	Pine green	217	319	1313
+	Dark pine green	218	890	1314

		ANCHOR	DMC	MADEIRA
♡	Purple	110	209	0803
K	Dark brown	1050	3781	1913
←	Light yellow	293	727	0110
⌐	Bright yellow	295	726	0100
∧	Pink	49	818	0404
Z	Black	403	310	Black
/	Grey blue	850	926	1707
V	Grass green	261	3052	1401
⌐	Grey ^	398	318	1802
\	Grey*	398	318	1802

Note: Bks window details of second house on left with cream. Bks window details of third house from left with black. Bks all other details with dark brown. Work grey ^ in cross stitch with one strand. Work grey in tent stitch with one strand.*

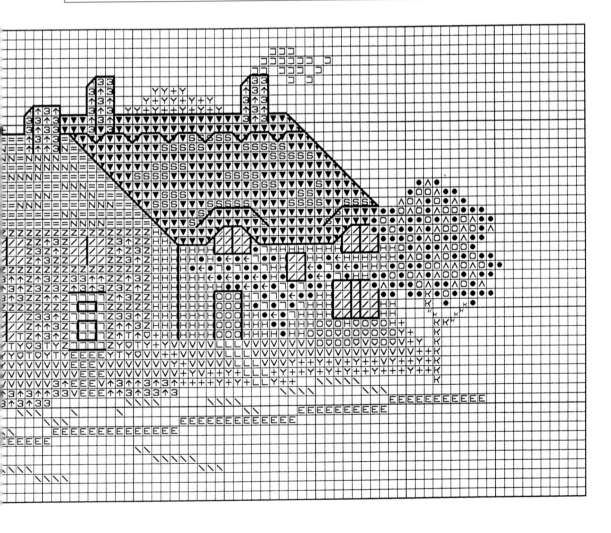

Cottage Garden Cushion

This lovely cushion shows a pretty cottage set in spacious gardens full of traditional cottage garden plants, together with a dove cote, a pond and a trellis festooned with roses.

COTTAGE GARDEN CUSHION

YOU WILL NEED

For the Cushion, with a design area of 19cm x
14cm (7¹/₂in x 5¹/₂in):

*50cm (20in) square of bone, 25-count
evenweave fabric*
*Stranded embroidery cotton in the colours
given in the panel*
No24 and No26 tapestry needles
Matching fabric for back of cushion
Needle and light-coloured sewing thread
40cm (16in) cushion pad

•

THE EMBROIDERY

Prepare the fabric, basting the horizontal and vertical centre lines, following the instructions given on
page 4. Set the fabric in a hoop or frame, and begin
stitching from the centre, following the chart.

Work the cross stitch over two threads of fabric

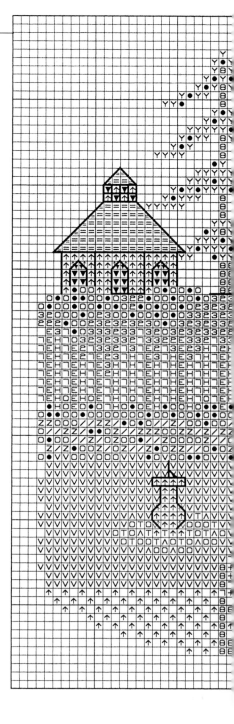

▶COTTAGE GARDEN CUSHION	ANCHOR	DMC	MADEIRA
⊟ White	01	Blanc	White
E Dark purple	111	208	0804
H Light purple	109	210	0802
T Red	19	347	0407
2 Brick	883	3064	2312
3 Dark brick	349	301	2306
O Dark grey green	216	367	1312
• Medium grey green	215	320	1311
= Brown	357	975	2303
N Chestnut	352	300	2304
↑ Sand	372	738	2013
Y Light grey green	859	523	1509
+ Dark green	218	890	1314
⊓ Medium purple	110	209	0803
8 Dark brown	1050	3781	1913
Z Light yellow	293	727	0110
/ Bright yellow	295	726	0100
∧ Pink	49	818	0404
▼ Grey blue	850	926	1707
V Grass green	265	3348	1409
L Rich grass green	266	3347	1408
⊐ Pale blue	920	932	1710
Very dark brown*	381	838	1914

Note: Bks details with very dark brown (*used for backstitch
only). See the separate chart for window detail.*

using two strands of thread in the No24 tapestry
needle. Make sure that all the top stitches run in the
same direction. Work the backstitch details using
one strand of thread and the No26 needle.

FINISHING

Remove the embroidery from the frame. Gently
hand wash the embroidery if desired. Press on the
reverse side with a warm steam iron. Ensuring that

the design is central, trim 3cm (1¼in) off each side of the fabric so that it measures 44cm (17½in) square. Place the cushion front and back together with right sides facing. Stitch around three sides, and the corners of the fourth side, 2cm (¾in) in from the edge. Neaten the raw edges either by oversewing, or by machine zig-zag stitch. Press, and turn the cover the right side out. Insert the cushion pad and slipstitch the remaining side closed.

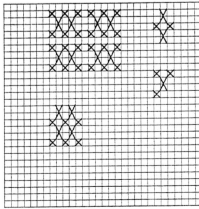

▶ *Backstitch window design*

Cottage Sampler

This attractive sampler, which is delicately edged with beaded flowers, features a traditional thatched cottage, with its long colourful front garden behind a picket fence. Two cats play in the garden path.

COTTAGE SAMPLER

YOU WILL NEED

For the Sampler, with a design area of 19cm x 16cm (7¹/₂in x 6¹/₄in):

40cm x 35.5cm (16in x 14¹/₄in) of pink, 14-count Aida fabric
Stranded embroidery cotton in the colours given in the panel
No24 and No26 tapestry needles
Strong thread, for lacing across the back
Cardboard for mounting
Frame of your choice

●

THE EMBROIDERY

Prepare the fabric, basting the horizontal and vertical centre lines, following the instructions given on page 4. Set the fabric in a hoop or frame, and begin stitching from the centre, following the chart. Ensure that the long axis of the fabric is running vertically.

Work the cross stitch using two strands of thread in the No24 needle. Make sure that all the top stitches run in the same direction. Work the backstitch details using one strand of thread and the No26 needle. Sew on the beads with the No26 needle and one strand of light pink cotton, using the second step of the cross stitch so that the beads lie in the same direction as the cross stitches (see Basic Skills page 7).

FINISHING

Remove the embroidery from the frame. Gently hand wash the embroidery if desired. Press on the reverse side with a warm steam iron. Mount as shown in the Basic Skills section on page 7, following the instructions for heavier fabrics. Insert the mounted picture into the frame according to the manufacturer's instructions.

▶ COTTAGE SAMPLER	ANCHOR	DMC	MADEIRA
② Light pink	895	223	0812
③ Sand	373	3828	2102
E Dark sand	374	420	2103
H Dark pink	896	221	0811
L Dark grass green	266	3347	1408
• Yellow	295	726	0100
↑ Grass green	265	3348	1409
S Dark grey green	262	3051	1508
V Brick	883	3064	2312
⊓ Grey	399	747	1802
Z Dark bright green	268	3345	1406
+ Pale purple	117	341	0901
O Brown	1050	3781	1913
▼ Bright green	267	3346	1407
T White	01	Blanc	White
N Dark purple	118	340	0902
\ Pinkish lilac	108	210	0802
△ Black	403	310	Black
K Medium pink bead	Bead design No23 or DMC NoV1 05 778		

Note: Bks white cat with white, black cat with black, and house and birds in the sky with brown.

Four Little Cottages

These little cottages are colourful
and quick to complete. The versatile
designs are shown stitched as small
pictures and as bread cloths to
enhance baskets of bread for the
table. The designs could also be
used for greeting cards.

FOUR LITTLE COTTAGES

YOU WILL NEED

For each Picture, with a design area
of 7.5cm (3in) square:

*25cm (10in) square of pale blue, 14-count
Aida fabric
Stranded embroidery cotton in the colours
given in the panel
No24 and No26 tapestry needles
Cardboard and masking tape
Frame of your choice*

For each Bread Cloth, with a design area of 7cm
(2³/₄in) square:

*33cm (13¹/₄in) square of ivory, 28-count
evenweave fabric
Stranded embroidery cotton in the colours
given in the panel
No24 and No26 tapestry needles
Cream stranded embroidery cotton*

•

THE PICTURES

For each picture, prepare the fabric, basting horizontal and vertical lines in the fabric, following the instructions given on page 4. Set the fabric in a hoop and begin stitching from the centre, following the chart.

Work the cross stitch using two strands of thread in the No24 tapestry needle, stitching over one block of fabric. Make sure that all the top stitches run in the same direction. Work the backstitch using one strand of thread and the No26 needle.

When you have finished the stitching, remove the fabric from the frame. Gently hand wash the embroidery if desired. Press on the reverse side with a warm iron. Mount the picture as shown in the Basic Skills section on page 7, following the instructions for lightweight fabrics. Insert the mounted picture into the frame according to the manufacturer's instructions.

THE BREAD CLOTHS

For each cloth, prepare the fabric by measuring up 11cm (4³/₄in) diagonally from the bottom right corner of the fabric. This point is the centre of the chart; mark it with a pin. Set the fabric in a hoop and begin stitching from the marked point. Work the cross stitch in the same way as for the pictures working over two threads of the fabric in each direction for a cross stitch.

When you have finished the embroidery, remove the fabric from the frame. Complete the cloth by hemstitching the edges, following the instructions for the Cottage Garden Place Mat (see page 10).

▶ FOUR LITTLE COTTAGES		ANCHOR	DMC	MADEIRA
☒	White	01	Blanc	White
Z	Black	403	310	black
3	Light brick	882	3773	2313
↑	Dark brick	883	3064	2312
H	Grey	8581	646	1812
◻	Grey blue	850	926	1707
L	Pale sand	366	739	2013
8	Sand	373	3828	2102
⊿	Dark sand	943	3045	2103
N	Bright brown	371	433	2303
V	Pale bright green	241	954	1211
Y	Bright green	243	912	1213
K	Medium green	267	3346	1407
S	Dark green	268	3345	1406
▼	Purple	109	210	0802
T	Red	1006	815	0511
▽	Pale yellow	293	727	0110
⊟	Brown	358	433	2008
	Dark brown*	381	838	1914

Note: Bks window detail on black and white cottage in white, and roof detail in bright brown. Bks window detail on other picture in dark brown* (*used for backstitch only). Bks window details on cottages on cloths in red.

Christmas Cottage Decorations

These sparkling little cottages with their silver and gold windows and delicate tassel hangings will ensure you have a white Christmas and charm all your Yuletide visitors.

CHRISTMAS COTTAGE DECORATIONS

YOU WILL NEED
For the Set of four Cottage Decorations, each with a design area of approximately 5.5cm x 6.5cm (2¼in x 2½in):

43cm (17¼in) square of lilac, 28-count evenweave fabric
Stranded embroidery cotton in the colours given in the panel
Stranded silver and gold metallic thread
No24 and No26 tapestry needles
Lightweight interfacing
Thin card for mounting
60g (2oz) wadding
Double-sided sticky tape
Lilac embroidery cotton
Lilac sewing thread and needle
Pale gold beads (DMC V3 08 3046)
Pale silver beads (DMC V3 07 317)

•

THE EMBROIDERY
Cut the fabric into four squares. Prepare each square, basting the horizontal and vertical centre lines of each design, following the instructions on page 4. Set the fabric in a hoop or frame and begin stitching from the centre, following the chart.

Work the cross stitch using two strands of thread in the No24 needle, and working over two threads of the fabric in each direction to form a cross stitch. Make sure that all the top stitches run in the same direction. Work the backstitch using one strand of thread and the No26 needle.

MAKING UP
Remove the embroideries from the frame. Gently hand wash if desired and press on the reverse side with a warm iron. Iron the interfacing on to the back of the embroideries. Cut out four circles of thin card, each measuring 9cm (3½in) in diameter. Centring the design carefully, lightly pencil round the card circles on the back of the embroideries. Leave a seam allowance of 12mm (½in) and cut away excess fabric.

Cut four pieces of wadding to fit on to the card circles. Stick in place with a small piece of double-sided sticky tape. Place a card circle on the back of each embroidery, sandwiching the wadding. Run a tacking thread around the seam allowance and pull up the thread to gather round the card. Tie the threads to secure in place.

To prepare the backing cut four circles of card slightly smaller than the fronts. Cover these with toning fabric in the same way as the fronts, but omitting the wadding. Make a hanging loop with 25cm (10in) of lilac stranded embroidery cotton, and stitch it in place to the centre back of the embroidery fabric with one strand of the same cotton. Neatly slipstitch the fronts of the decorations to the backs with toning thread.

To complete each decoration, make a tassel with two 50cm (20in) pieces of gold, two of silver, and one of lilac stranded cotton. Fold these over once, then again. Stitch the looped end to the bottom of the embroidery in the centre. Wrap the lilac sewing thread around the tassel three or four times to form a head. Secure the thread with a small stitch around the wrapped threads at the back. Thread a few gold beads on to lilac threads and wrap these around the tassel once; secure again in the same way. Then thread a few silver beads on to lilac thread and make a second row in the same way. Fasten off the thread at the back of the tassel and trim the bottom to finish.

► COTTAGE DECORATIONS	ANCHOR	DMC	MADEIRA
• White	01	Blanc	White
⟍ Grey & brown	8581 & 358	646 & 433	1812 & 2008
S Light brick	882	3773	2313
T Dark brick	883	3064	2312
3 Brown	358	433	2008
V Gold & Silver	Gold lame 300 & Silver lame 301	Gold 5282 & Silver Argent	- -
H Dark green	263	520	1601
L Red	1005	815	0511

Note: Bks the windows to match the door of the decoration, either red or dark green. Bks around the cottages in white.

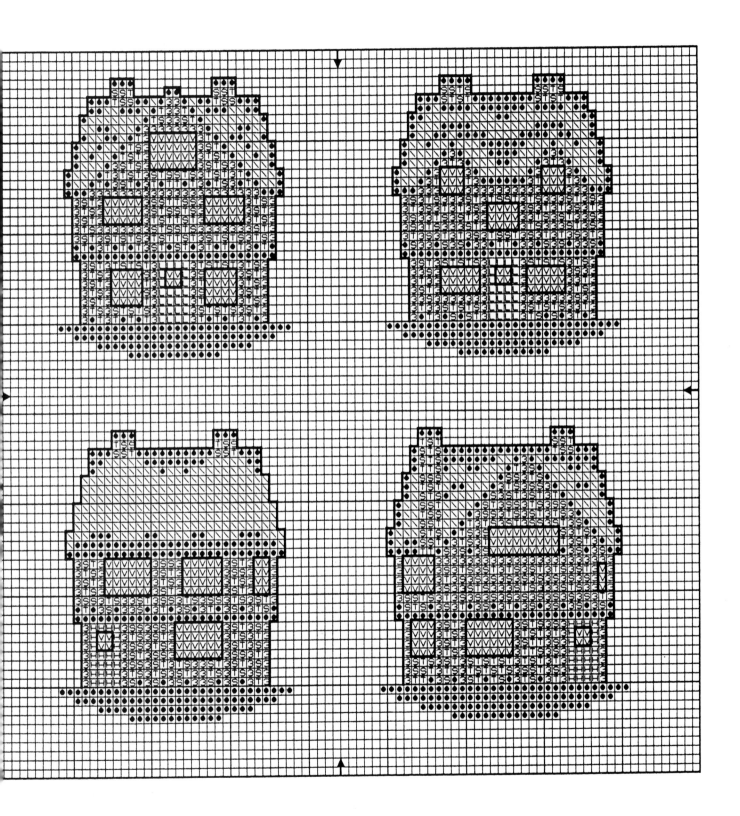

The Village

This colourful depiction of a country village in summer shows pretty cottages nestling in the steep hillside beside the church and the old ruined castle. The pavilion in the centre leads the eye around the lanes to the bridge over the stream, and to the old stocks in the foreground of the picture.

THE VILLAGE

YOU WILL NEED
For the Picture, with a design area of
23cm x 17cm (9¼in x 6¾in):

*46cm x 40cm (18¼in x 16in) of ivory,
14-count Aida fabric
Stranded embroidery cotton in the colours
given in the panel
No24 and No26 tapestry needles
Strong thread for lacing across the back
Cardboard for mounting
Frame of your choice*

•

THE EMBROIDERY

Prepare the fabric, basting the horizontal and vertical centre lines, following the instructions given on page 4. Set the fabric in a hoop or frame, and begin

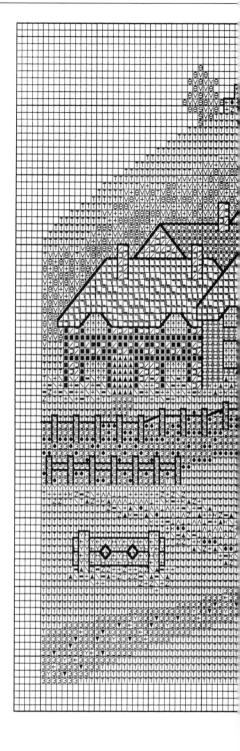

▶ THE VILLAGE		ANCHOR	DMC	MADEIRA
②	White	01	Blanc	White
③	Pale grey	900	648	1814
•	Medium grey	8581	646	1812
↑	Blue grey	850	926	1707
■	Black	403	310	Black
⊟	Cream	366	739	2013
⊔	Sand	373	3828	2102
⊓	Dark sand	374	420	2103
◯	Chestnut	351	301	2305
⑤	Brown	357	400	2304
⊤	Grass green	265	3348	1409
∨	Grey green	262	3051	1602
⑧	Dark green	263	520	1601
☒	Bright green	266	3347	1408
+	Medium bright green	267	3346	1407
⧄	Brick	883	3064	2312
⊐	Rust	349	301	2306
▲	Bright yellow	295	726	0100
▬	Red	19	347	0407
⧅	Purple	109	210	0802
⧄	Pale blue	920	932	1710
⊥	Medium blue	921	931	1711
▼	Grey brown	903	3022	1903
▽	Bright brown	371	434	2009
E	Dull pink	893	225	0814
←	Light stone	391	3024	1901
Y	Stone	392	3032	2002
K	Bright pink	50	3716	0606
	Very dark brown*	381	838	1914

Note: Bks castle, gate, church and fences in black, and all other outlines in very dark brown (*used for backstitch only).*

stitching from the centre, following the chart. Ensure that the long axis of the fabric runs horizontally.

Work the cross stitch using two strands of thread in the No24 needle, and over one block of the fabric. Make sure that all the top stitches run in the same direction. Work the backstitch using one strand of thread and the No26 needle.

FINISHING

Remove the embroidery from the frame. Gently hand wash the embroidery if desired. Press on the reverse side with a warm iron. Mount as shown in the Basic Skills section on page 7, following the instructions for heavier fabrics. Insert the mounted picture into the frame according to the manufacturer's instructions.

ACKNOWLEDGEMENTS

Many thanks to Coats Paton Crafts for supplying the threads and fabrics used throughout this book.

Thanks also to Framecraft Miniatures Ltd for the coasters, Bead Design for the embroidery beads, Katherine Blakey for the picture frames, and, last but not least, thanks to Jackie Williams for the cushion pad.

Special thanks are also due to my team of diligent stitchers: Tracy Medway, Ann Swetman, Elizabeth Hatton, and Ann Baldwin.

SUPPLIERS

Katherine Blakey
Picture Frame Workshop
8 Sandford Avenue
Church Stretton
Shropshire
SY6 6BW
Telephone: 01694 723334

Addresses for framecraft stockists worldwide
Framecraft Miniatures
Limited
372/376 Summer Lane
Hockley
Birmingham B19 3QA
England
Telephone: 0121 212 0551

Ireland Needlecraft Pty Ltd
2-4 Kepple Drive
Hallam
Victoria 3803
Australia

Danish Art Needlework
PO Box 442, Lethbridge
Alberta TIJ 3Z1
Canada

Sanyei Imports
PO Box 5, Hashima Shi
Gifu 501-62
Japan

The Embroidery Shop
286 Queen Street
Masterton
New Zealand

Anne Brinkley Designs Inc.
246 Walnut Street
Newton
Mass. 02160
USA

S A Threads and Cottons Ltd
43 Somerset Road
Cape Town
South Africa

For information on your nearest stockist of embroidery cotton, contact the following:

DMC
(also distributors of Zweigart fabrics)
UK
DMC Creative World
Limited
62 Pullman Road, Wigston
Leicester LE8 2DY
Telephone: 01162 2811040

USA
The DMC Corporation
Port Kearney Bld.
10 South Kearney
NJ 07032-0650
Telephone: 201 589 0606

AUSTRALIA
DMC Pty Ltd
PO Box 317
Earlwood
NSW 2206
Telephone: 02 9559 3088

COATS AND ANCHOR
UK
Coats Paton Crafts
McMullen Road
Darlington
Co. Durham DL1 1YQ
Telephone: 01325 394242

USA
Coats & Clark
PO Box 24998
Greenville SC 29616
Telephone: 800 243 0810

AUSTRALIA
Coats Spencer Crafts
Level 1, 382 Wellington Rd
Mulgrave
Victoria 3170
Telephone: 03 9561 2288

MADEIRA
UK
Madeira Threads (UK) Ltd
Thirsk Industrial Park
York Road, Thirsk
N. Yorkshire YO7 3BX
Telephone: 01845 524880

USA
Madeira Marketing Ltd
600 East 9th Street
Michigan City
IN 46360
Telephone: 219873 1000

AUSTRALIA
Penguin Threads Pty Ltd
25-27 Izett Street
Prahran
Victoria 3181
Telephone: 03 9529 4400